The Orchard Book of Starry Tales

For Lucian Clinch
Geraldine McCaughrean

For Leo
Sophy Williams

Orchard Books
96 Leonard Street, London EC2A 4RH
Orchard Books, Australia
14 Mars Road, Lane Cove, NSW 2066
Text © Geraldine McCaughrean 1998
Illustrations © Sophy Williams 1998
ISBN 1 86039 108 7
First published in Great Britain in 1998
The rights of Geraldine McCaughrean to be identified as the Author
and Sophy Williams to be identified as the Illustrator of this Work
has been asserted by them in accordance with the
Copyright, Designs and Patents Act 1998
A CIP catalogue record of this book is available
from the British Library
Printed in Hong Kong / China

The Orchard Book of
Starry Tales

☆ Retold by Geraldine McCaughrean ☆

☆ Illustrated by Sophy Williams ☆

ORCHARD BOOKS

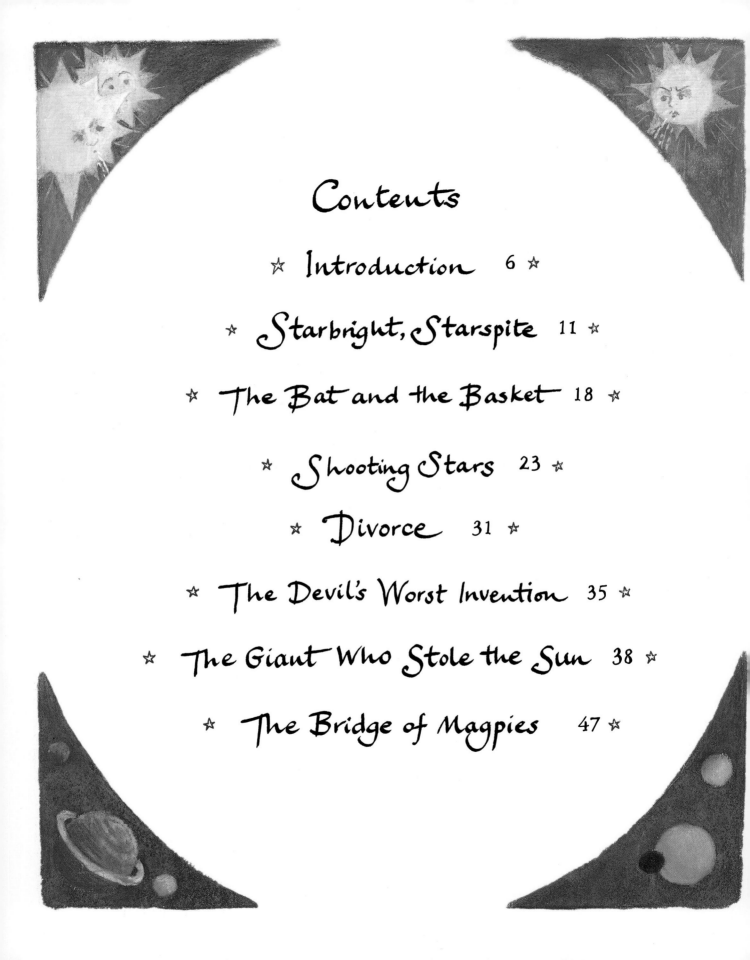

Contents

Introduction

What do you see when you look up at night? The Inuits see a million glittering little ponds and lakes puddling a grassy plain. Other peoples see holes in a solid black vault, others diamonds stitched to cloth. And what of the patterns those stars make?

The human brain strives always to 'recognise' shapes and objects already in its memory banks. And so it sees pictures within the random scatter of glowing lights – men and women, monsters, ships and castles and trees. It is the brain's way – it is *our* way – of making order out of chaos. And people have been doing it for thousands of years.

Nowadays, in the West, few look to the sky in all earnest for advice. But, to those who can read its language, the sky still has very real advice to give – not predictions or warnings of disaster, but practical navigational guidance for sailors and a sky-wide clock face marking the passage of seasons; it tells farmers when to plant, when to expect the rains.

You will find signs of the celestial Zodiac in the horoscope pages of many magazines and newspapers. But there are hundreds of other constellations with names – and myths to account for those names. What one culture sees as a plough, another sees as a saucepan, another as a bear; what to one is a circle of chiefs sitting

at pow-wow, another calls a string of money, another a bride's crown of flowers. The Greek Orion is the war-god Skanda in India, Algebar the giant in Arabia, General Xeng in China. Our Sagittarius was the Mesopotamian Scorpion-man guarding the Gates of Hell. Cancer the Crab was Ancient Egypt's divine scarab beetle, rolling the Sun towards the Portals of Dawn. For most, the Milky Way is the road taken by the Dead as they set out for the Afterlife.

It is rather comforting to think of our forebears looking down over us, of God using the canvas sky to paint large the deeds of mortal heroes. It makes little Earth seem important in the universal scheme of things – more than a mere rock amid empty, howling Space.

And even though man-made lighting has tried to push Night away to a safe distance, even though it has made the stars harder to see, it is still possible to stand outdoors, in a hail of dizzying stars, and spot constellations, exactly as our ancestors did. It is still possible to enjoy the stories those stars have generated.

When you do look up, consider this. The light from some of those stars has travelled for so long to get here that the star itself has burned out, gone. What are you looking at, then? The memory of a star? Its ghost? Its story written in light?

Starbright, Starspite

A North American Indian Story

HERE at the beginning, let us speak of the beginnings, when the Creator of the World hung up Sun and Moon in the sky and played jacks with the Stars, tossing and catching them on the back of his great hand. When he tired of playing, he hammered home all but a handful, to nail the heavens in place. And between his palms he idly shaped a ball of bald, bare clay.

Before parting for opposite ends of the sky, Sun and Moon married and had a child – a boy – and set him down feet-first on the bald, bare Earth. Before travelling to their solitary outposts, two Stars also married, and had a child – a girl – and set her down feet-

11

first on the bald, bare Earth. Boy and girl met, of course, and they married, too.

Seeing that the planet he had shaped was now inhabited, Great God Tirawa held council with his ministers of light and said: "Sun! Light the way for those two small people, and warm their days.

"Moon! Bind their eyes in sleep each night with your gentle rays, and give them sweet dreams.

"Stars! I give you charge of the elements, the clouds and wind and rain, to shape the landscape for this First Man and First Woman," said Tirawa to his favourite Stars.

"Starbright! While this work goes on, I give my wallet of tools into your safekeeping, since only you are wise and mighty enough to be trusted with it.

"Now, my bright jacks, go down to Earth and teach First Man and First Woman all they need to know."

So the Stars taught First Man how to hunt and survive and defend his family, and how to worship Great God Tirawa. And they taught First Woman how to plant and harvest and cook food for her family, and how to worship Great God Tirawa.

Perhaps there was too much to remember. Perhaps the work took up too much of their time. But First Man and First Woman soon forgot to worship Tirawa or to thank him for their planet. And though their family had grown now to thousands of sons and daughters, grandchildren and great-grandchildren, Tirawa lost his love of the small people on Earth.

"Starburn! To whom did I entrust the thunderclouds?" he asked, making the Universe quake with his anger.

"To me, O Great God Tirawa."

"Then kindle the Earth with lightning and let it *burn*!"

It was no sooner said than done. A forked firebrand of lightning flashed, and the dry grass kindled to a sea of running flame, trees bursting into torches of fire. Gone were the crops of First Woman, the traps of First Man. Gone were their great-grandchildren, grandchildren and children, their houses, their beds. Gone was all trace of them from the face of the Earth.

Or so it seemed.

"Star-of-the-Rainclouds," commanded Tirawa. "The smoke of my destruction chokes me. Wash it away and let the fires cease!"

So Star-of-the-Rainclouds pierced the clouds with his sharp spurs, and let the rain fall in cataracts over the charred world. Now floods rolled cold and deep, black with ash, washing clean the bald, bare Earth. Then Star-Windraiser loosed winds to dry up the flood, and everything was as it had been before the marriage of Sun and Moon and Stars.

Or so it seemed.

Out of a cave at the top of a high cliff crept a little old man and a little old woman. He carried a tobacco pipe, a smouldering twig and a drum – all that he had saved from the fire and floods. She carried a cob of corn and a handful of pumpkin seeds.

"Well, husband, where shall we begin?" she said.

When Great God Tirawa saw the spirit and determination of Pawnee Man and Pawnee Woman, he smiled and held back his thunderbolts and meteorites, his catastrophes and disasters.

"Let them live and prosper for ever," he said with sudden surge of loving pride in Humankind.

Unfortunately he had not reckoned with jealousy.

Oh, it was not Pawnee Man or Pawnee Woman who were jealous. They had long since learned to be content, to respect the gods, and to teach their children humility and hard work. No, it was not the small people of Earth who were jealous. It was the Stars.

Greatest and brightest of the Star jacks, Starbright, had been entrusted by Tirawa with his wallet of tools. And yet all she had done with it was to hang it on the topmost branch of the tallest tree on the highest hill on Earth. She had not so much as opened the bag to look inside.

"If Tirawa had given *me* his toolbag, I wouldn't have left it lying idle," complained Starspite to himself, his silver light turning lemon yellow with bitterness and sour envy. "*I* would have put the tools to good use. Starbright wants to keep them all to herself. Either that or she's too stupid to know what to do with them!"

So Starspite swooped on the tall pine tree, unlooped the cords of the bag from the topmost branches, and let it spill its contents.

Hailstones and thunderbolts, sleet and storms of meteorites fell to Earth like the end of the world. Reptilian purple winds, and coils of sulphurous whirlwind ripped the leaves from the trees and soured the water in the ponds. Sandstorms and hurricanes flattened crops and forests. And Starspite's silver shine was scoured to a dull steely grey by flying grit.

They were not Tirawa's tools of creation in the bag, but his tools of destruction.

As quickly as it had begun, the cataclysm died away. The serpents of ice wriggled into holes in the ground. The birds of oily blackness roosted in hollow trees, out of sight. The verminous whistles and hoots squirmed in among the debris of the storm. Starspite looked this way and that, to see if anyone had seen his awful mistake. And when no one came running, he sneaked away, relieved that nothing worse had befallen Tirawa's creation.

But from that day onward men began to fall sick, women to grow old, children to drown, babies to cry. And cry. And cry. For accidents lurked now on cliff ledges and in the rivers. Illness had roosted in the hollow trees. Old age had soaked into the ground. Sadness and bad luck had burrowed under the houses of Humankind. In short, Death had escaped from Tirawa's toolbag, and there was no recapturing it – no more than the seeds blown from a dandelion.

When the Pawnee people found out how Starspite had poisoned their paradise, they picked up stones and pelted the night sky. The Stars were obliged to move off, farther off, carrying the sky with them higher and higher up.

Otherwise we would see them as they really are, close to – as large as the sun which warms us or the moon which binds up our eyes at night with milk-white dreams.

The Bat and the Basket

A Kono Myth from Sierra Leone

WHEN the world was made but not peopled, lit but lived in only by animals, their night was as light as day, for the Moon shone as bright as the Sun. The night sky was as blue as cornflowers, and nothing but the spreading trees and purple thunderclouds cast a welcome patch of shade.

Then one day God asked his animal creations, "Who will go up to the House of the Moon, and deliver this basket for me?"

"Not I," said the eagle. "The brightness of the Moon dazzles my eyes." And the same was true for all the birds, because the Moon blazed, incandescent.

"I will go," said Mr Bat. "I am blind, and the brightness won't trouble me."

So God entrusted to Mr Bat a large covered basket woven from strange reeds, which did not rattle when it was shaken and which weighed no more than a handful of feathers. God did not mention what was inside. Mr Bat stretched his wide wings, hooked the basket on to one of the claws at the leathery wingfold, and flew off towards the Moon.

But though the basket was light, it was awkward to carry. After a time, Mr Bat changed it over to the other wing, and flew on. After a few miles more, he looped one handle round his neck and flew on. But by the time he reached the brow of Moonshine Hill, directly below the Moon, he was tired out. Hungry as well. He set the basket down while he went cruising to and fro, sipping insects off the wind.

Certain animals came trotting over the crest of the hill. First a fox picked up the basket to see if it was heavy with good things to eat. But it weighed no more than a handful of feathers. "Must be empty," he said.

A cow came by, and, hooking up the basket on one horn, shook

it, to see if it was full of grain. But when it did not rattle she dropped it again, so that the lid was jarred loose.

An anteater came along and, finding a gap just wide enough for his long nose, poked it inside, to see if the basket was full of ants. But all he sniffed was a vaporous, dank sort of smell, and he left the basket alone, the lid pushed a little farther aside.

Along came a monkey with clever paws, who could slip her long fingers down the side of the lid and grope about. Perhaps the basket was full of bananas! But all she felt was a cold clamminess, so she pulled out her paw. She even put the lid back on tight.

Along came an elephant. Did not even see the basket. It was he who kicked it over and sent the round lid bowling away, he who spilled the contents over Moonshine Hill.

Suddenly a column of smoky dark funnelled upwards and engulfed the Moon, smearing its bright face with smuts and smudges of sooty dark. Her bright beams withered like the petals of a flower blasted by frost. She turned from gold to tarnished silver.

All at once the hill was shrouded in darkness – the first darkness the world had ever known. This was not dappled like the shade beneath the trees, not grey like when clouds hid the sun. This was a thick, treacly, dense, impenetrable blackness such that the elephant could not see the end of his trunk, the monkey could not see as far as the banana trees, the anteater could see no stirring of black insects along the black, black ground. The cow stopped stock still. The black pupils of the fox's yellow eyes dilated, like two tiny moons.

Whatever God's plans had been for the basket of dark, they were now all undone. Mr Bat, returning to complete the trip, fluttered

into a swelling cloud of gloom. "Oh no! Oh no!" he cried, and his voice came out shrill with horror, shriller than a bird's song, shriller than a whistle – so high, in fact that human ears cannot hear it. This way and that sped Mr Bat, trying to scoop the darkness back into the basket: "Oh no! Oh no! Oh no!"

He tries every night. Every evening as the Sun sets and the Moon rises and dark steals over the Earth, the million grandchildren of Mr Bat flitter out of their caves and try to capture the dark, to gather it back into the basket where God placed it. But it is too large for them, too flapping. They may go on trying for ever.

Shooting Stars
An Arabian Story

BEFORE there was an Earth to walk on, Allah, the One God, made the angels out of light. He made other spirits, too. Before there was one grain of sand in the Sahara Desert, God made the frightening shaitans out of fire. And before one grain of desert sand ever blew into the eye of a man (for this was long before Mankind), God made the djinn. He took the burning wind that scours and scorches the desert, and knotted it into ifrits or djinn, creatures of beautiful magic and magical beauty.

Transparent as glass, shape-shifting and cunning as riverwater, the djinn could be as large as a solar system, as small as a pinprick. Their King was Jinn ben Jann, and under his rule the marvellous

cities of Chilminar and Baalbek were built, each with forty towers
spiralling towards the sky. Among their mazy alleyways lurked the
hosts of djinn, whispering, whispering that no power in the world
was greater than the power of the djinn.

One djinn, more beautiful than all the rest, travelled to Heaven
at the invitation of God, and there he led the life of an angel, saw
wonders which made Chilminar and Baalbek seem squalid and
small. His name was Azazel, and God grew very fond of him.

But when, one day, Azazel glanced out of Heaven and saw Jinn
ben Jann mustering his troops, he watched with a smile on his lips.
He did not fly to warn God, did not yell a warning or swing on the
bells of Heaven to sound the alarm. Azazel simply folded his fingers
inside his fists and whispered, "Yes, yes. Attack!"

Their shapes all distorted into the most hideous ghouls, demons
and monsters, the rebellious djinn attacked. But God, too, had seen
them coming, for God sees everything. An army of angels three
thousand legions deep closed ranks behind Allah, the One God.
The sky turned red, the sea ran blood-red, but the hosts of Heaven
and Earth fought on in pitched battle at the fringes of the sky.
Hand to hand through the streets of Baalbek the angels fought the
djinn. The forty towers of Chilminar burned. And Jinn ben Jann,
along with most of his race of djinn, paid with his life for his pride
and ambition.

"Traitor!" cried God, catching hold of Azazel by the shimmering
hair.

"Who, me?" Azazel protested. "But I was here all the time!
What have I done, Lord, that you should be angry with me?"

"Nothing but watch. I cherished you like a son, taught you truths and showed you love. But you stood by and watched while the angels bled. So, get out! Go! And never again climb this high. In future keep to the low places of your birth!"

Azazel fell for thirty days, and as he fell he cursed God. Landing with a splash as large as a blue whale, he found that he was not entirely alone on the blue-green Earth. Other djinn had survived the slaughter, and were dragging themselves ashore, on to an island in the Indian Ocean. Most were as ugly now as they had been beautiful before, terrible to look at, hideous to smell or hear or contemplate. They sat down beneath the date palms and chewed on their discontent. Azazel made himself King of the Djinn, and he bided, bided his time…

Horribly deceived in his beautiful creation, God created instead the Human Race, and though they too disappointed and disobeyed him, God did not send his angel troops to destroy them. After all, some at least were

good, brave and God-fearing. Some were kind
and honest and wise.

King Solomon was wise – some say he was the wisest
man who ever lived – because when God offered to grant
him one wish, Solomon did not ask for wealth or fame: he
asked simply for wisdom.

In answer to Solomon's prayer, God sent an angel with two gifts
– a ring engraved with God's secret, unspoken name, and a carpet
of green silk. When the carpet was unrolled, there was room on it
for Solomon's throne and all his household. All the courtiers and
armed forces stood to the right of the throne while on the left stood
the spirits. For Solomon's ring gave him power of command over
the djinn.

"Fetch me the libraries of Baalbek, the writings of Chilminar!"
Solomon would tell them. "Fetch me the Queen of Sheba!" And the
djinn had to obey, because God's name imparted such magic to the
ring. Only Azazel had more.

What a sight it must have been to see that vast silk carpet rise
into the air, bearing Solomon on his throne up, up into the sky.
The birds spread their wings and flocked overhead – a canopy of
feathers iridescent with colours and brilliant with song. Solomon
flew out into space as far as the celestial spheres and there, perched
like a sparrow on a wire, he learned the secrets of the Universe.

He learned the language of animals and where the daylight ends;
he saw to the end of infinity and rode inside the atom. He alone
was allowed through the little gate of Heaven, and looked down
from its towers at Earth. And he saw the djinn making mischief.

For instance, they would drop pebbles from roofs
on to passers-by; steal food from a man's plate when his back was
turned; tempt women away from their families by disguising
themselves as cakes, jewels, lovers; frighten children by pulling faces
at their windows; steal bodies from graveyards…

So Solomon had ten thousand bottles made and, by the power of
his ring, commanded the djinn to clean inside each bottle. (Only
Azazel did not come when he was called, did not, would not, do as
he was bid.) Their eyes bulged at Solomon, green through the glass,
noses squashed flat. And Solomon sealed each bottle with wax,
imprinting the seal with the ring's engraving – King Solomon's Seal
– then threw them into the Indian Ocean to bob about for eternity.
A thousand years of sea-sickness. A thousand years adrift in those
chilly, grass-green cells of glass, the only excitement the passing
of a fish.

But every once in a while a fishing net would haul up a catch, and there, tangled in the mesh, would be a harmless-looking bottle. King Solomon was long-since dead, though the stories of his magic lived on. Some fishermen wisely threw back their catch. But others either forgot the story of King Solomon's Seal, or gave in to the pleading voice within the bottle.

"Let me out! Please let me out! How could a poor little maltreated chap like me possibly do you any harm? And think of the reward!"

"What will you give me if I release you?" asked one greedy fisherman.

"More money than you can spend, fame longer than a lifetime – everything you deserve!" promised the djinn inside the bottle.

And so the fisherman broke Solomon's Seal, and out around his hand flowed green and purple wisps of smoke, a stream of sparks, an indescribable smell. Larger than the fisherman, larger than his boat, larger than the clouds overhead, large as the sky itself, the djinn unfurled himself in breaking free. And there, scimitar in hand, astride the sea, the djinn would bellow with laughter until the sea bed quaked. He struck off the head of the foolish fisherman – just as he deserved – and swirled away into the purpling sky, shrieking, "Free! Free! Free at last!"

Azazel had told his djinn all that he had seen in Paradise as he studied alongside the angels, and now the djinn hunger and thirst to see with their own eyes the crystal spires, the sea of glass, the thrones of light, all the colours of perfect bliss. It has become their sole object in life to climb up and up the hills of night, to peep over

the walls of Heaven, to glimpse the Paradise lost to them for ever when they rebelled against God.

Perhaps they think to burrow under the crystal walls, to creep in like ants and bite the ankles of the blessed, or to storm the citadel and set Azazel on God's throne of light.

Consequently, the angels are always on their guard, always walking the walls of Heaven, armoured in light. At the first sight of a creeping, stealthy djinn, the alarm is raised and the angels hurl down spears and fiery brands, fragments of broken stars, and white-hot words. Dazzled and scorched, terrified and turning tail, the djinn lose their balance on the slippery ledges of the sky, and plummet back to Earth.

Shooting stars we call them, that fusillade of angel spearpoints and firebrands. Some people see a shooting star and make a wish. But the only wish we should ever probably make is that the troops of Azazel never, never take the angels unaware, and break through the walls of Heaven.

Divorce

☆

A Story from Togo, West Africa

SUN and Moon married and had many, many children. You could count them all if it were possible to count all the stars. But Sun and Moon could not agree about anything – what to call the children, how to bring them up, which crops to grow or where to sleep, how many pails of rain to spill on the Earth below, or where to go swimming in the evening sea.

So Sun and Moon parted, he to live at one end of the sky, she to live at the other, and now they do their best to avoid each other. Some of the children chose to stay with their father, others left with their mother. Everything the couple owned – every wedding present and nick-nack – the quarrelling parents divided up between them.

31

"You take Mars."

"I'll have Mercury."

"Some of those meteorites are mine."

"The comets are yours, and welcome."

"One for you. One for me."

Such arguments are never settled peaceably. Even after the divorce, Moon brooded on the size of her share, and complained. She compared Sun's fields of blue with hers of black, and felt cheated. That is why sometimes she goes back.

Her footsteps drift back towards her husband's property, and she walks through the blue fields of Daytime – you may have seen her – when, by rights, she should keep to her own black acres. Her children go with her, of course, clutching at her skirts or somersaulting along behind. And if Sun's children happen to be out playing in the fields, the most dreadful squabbles break out. Brother and sister jeer and thumb their noses, carrying on the fight their parents began:

"Night's better than Day! Nah-nah-nah-nah!"

"'Tisn't, 'tisn't! Who's afraid of the dark, then? Nah-nah-nah-nah-nah!"

They start to throw stones, or handfuls of dirt. Worst of all, they try to spit in one another's eyes – stars who used to live happily together as brother and sister!

Down here on the Earth, a farmer wipes his forehead and holds out a hand. Rain? Naturally. It's always the same when the Moon comes out before nightfall.

But inwardly Moon hates to see her children fight. It breaks her heart. The rain that falls at such times is not so much the spitting

of the stars as the tears of Mother Moon watching her beloved children brawl and row. So out from the front of her dress she pulls a long banner and, waving it over her head, she calls for peace.

"Hush now, children! That's enough. Be still. Aren't we all one family, your father, yourselves and I? Just because we live apart these days, does it mean we have to wrangle like a flock of ducks and geese? Make friends now. Kiss and make up."

The children turn towards her, thumbs creeping into their weary mouths. Their eyes are held enthralled, fascinated by the banner of pretty cloth she holds – the brilliant colourful, billowy gauzy scarf, the rainbow blowing itself to tatters above their mother's calling face.

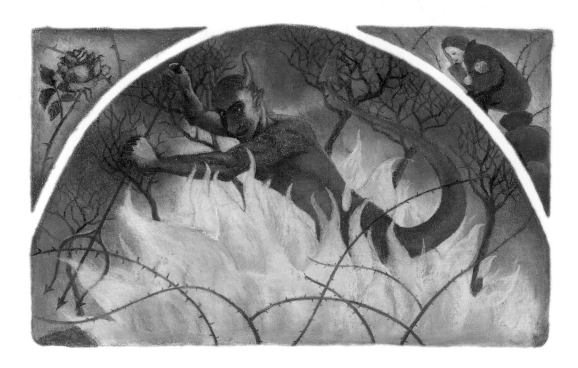

The Devil's Worst Invention
A French Folktale

WHEN the world was new-made and perfect, before the first tear had fallen in sorrow, the Devil saw all the happiness there was, and flinched from the brightness of it. "I see," he snarled. "So God loves his puny *people*, does he? In that case, I shall spoil their lives and give them some reason to hate him!"

He covered the smooth stem of the rose with stabbing thorns, spiked the blackberry cane, hung burs on the burdock, spines on the porcupine. In short he made a prickly curse.

But the people did not stop loving God because of illness and blight. So the Devil had to think again. "I'll plant nightmares in their sleep like the seeds of weeds, whittle disappointments sharp enough to pierce their little hearts." In short, he made a bitter curse. Tireless in his spite, he went on and on marring God's creation. "Mud and leeches in their washing water, rocks to break the ploughshare, weevils in the cotton…"

Suddenly the Devil broke off. A new invention, worse than any yet, had just crept into his fevered brain: a terrible machine, an appalling siege engine, a new and ultimate weapon in his war! Without a moment's delay, he began to kick the hills to pieces, and to gather the noise of it into a sack. With his trident he stampeded the monsters of the Underworld, and captured the sound of their running hooves. He took all the rattles and tins and drums, all the volcanoes and avalanches, and welded them together with a club hammer. Then he wrapped the whole thing in midnight – and there it was: the world's first roll of THUNDER.

It was loud – lake-shaking, earth-quaking loud. Only one noise in the universe was louder. That was the voice of God saying, "NO!" At that, even the Devil covered his scarlet ears.

"*Thus far and no farther!*" said God. "Have I not watched you make your curses, prickly, bitter and cruel, without lifting one finger to stop you? I knew that the rose's thorns would only make it more prized; the hard labour of our harvest would only make bread more delicious. Your wickedness will only drive the people closer and closer to me. But your thunder I will not tolerate! That I will not allow!"

"How are you going to stop me?" jeered the Devil, pulling a face and thumbing his nose at Heaven.

"Oh, I am not," replied God more calmly. "Do your worst! I shall simply send my spear ahead of your thunder – for a warning." And he took his spear and scorched the Devil's breeches with it – drove him off the sky with a blade of light so sharp it slashed through the very fabric of Night.

Now, though the Devil still hurls his thunderbolts out of the dark of his hiding place, God keeps eternal watch for them. Always in time, he throws his spear of golden light. Faster than the thunder it flies, flashing like a beacon, warning like a lighthouse beam, flickering against sleeping lashes. People have time to wake and cover their ears with their hands, their heads with a pillow. Because lightning always arrives ahead of thunder. You just see if it isn't true.

The Giant Who Stole the Sun
A Story from Afghanistan

The giant Espereg, whose fortress stood amid the impenetrable mountain ranges of the Hindu Kush, wandered from room to room shaking his hoary head. A million candles burned on the sills, and torches flamed in their sconces, but the place was still gloomy. Though he had employed artists and craftsmen to decorate each ceiling and wall, their artistry went unseen for want of light. Even the waterfall built at the centre of the fortress, foaming and tinkling and cool, was sunk in shadow.

So Espereg went out and stole the Sun and Moon.

In those days both Sun and Moon burned in three-legged iron beacon-baskets on the top of twin mountain peaks in the Hindu

Kush. When Espereg came home
with them tucked under his coat,
his mother asked, "What have you got there, Espereg?"

And Espereg answered, "An orange tree and a lemon
tree to stand either side of my waterfall."

That is where he put them: the Sun on the right,
the Moon on the left. And the golden
fortress was filled with sudden
light, its carvings illuminated,
its fountains awash with
diamonds of brightness. That
pleased Espereg who had a great
hunger for beauty.

☆

"What's that noise?"

"Who's there?"

"I can't see you."

"So cold."

"SOMEONE HAS STOLEN THE SUN!"

"Even the night is not this dark!"

"WELL THEN, SOMEONE HAS STOLEN
THE MOON, TOO!"

Outside the golden fortress, the world from Pole to
Pole was plunged into utter darkness and bitter cold.

"Help us, Mandi! Help us!" cried
the people of the world, and
the god Mandi resolved to
rescue the Moon and Sun.

Not strong enough to fight the giant, Mandi knew he must use cunning to get inside the fortress. So he turned himself into a little boy – an amazingly beautiful child – and knocked at the gleaming door.

No sooner had Espereg laid eyes on the boy than he wanted him for his own son. Such was his hunger for all things beautiful. Mandi noticed how the giant himself had turned quite golden in the Sun and Moon light. His mother too.

"This is going to be easy," said Mandi to himself as the giant bounced him on his knees.

Not a bit of it!

Next day, before Espereg went out to tend his goats, he shut his newly adopted son in the cellar. "No one shall rob you from me, pretty boy, and you won't come to no harm," said the giant, gently placing the child, with finger and thumb, at the bottom of the cellar steps. "Grandma will feed you, little toodle-eggy-bumps, and Daddy will soon be home again."

Now Mandi had a horror of dark places – darkness sapped him of strength. Here, too, was his only chance to find the Sun and Moon and sneak them out of the fortress. So as soon as the giant had gone, Mandi ran up the cellar steps and leaned his shoulder against the door.

It was huge. It was heavy. It was locked.

He pushed and he strained and he heaved. The door bowed outwards a tiny fraction – just enough for Mandi to poke one finger through the gap. Then his strength failed, and he had to snatch his hand back inside. One finger was stained gold by the Sun and Moon light outside.

"What you been a-doin' of, little legalump?" said the giant's mother when she came to give him his lunch. "You been a-tryin' to get out? My Espereg wouldn't like that. My Espereg would eat you up if he thought you was a-tryin' to get loose."

Mandi decided to tell her everything. "Your son has stolen the Sun and Moon, and the world is lost without them!"

"Ah," said the giant's mother. Nothing more. But she bandaged Mandi's golden finger so that Mandi should not get into trouble with the giant.

Next day Espereg went out to tend his goats. Before he left, he shut Mandi in the cellar again. "Gotta keep you safe, little poogie-flugle buttonchop. Don't you go a-cuttin' no more fingers, you hear?"

Soon as he was gone, Mandi walked up the cellar steps (the darkness sapped his strength) and beat and battered at the door until it opened a crack wider than before. Out shot Mandi's arm. But though he fumbled for the latch, he could not free it. And when he pulled in his arm again, exhausted, the whole length of it was shining yellow from the Sun and Moon light.

"What you been a-doin' of, little bulgy bodikin?" said the giant's mother when she brought him his food.

41

Mandi decided to throw himself on her mercy. "Your son has helped himself to the Sun and Moon and now the world is all over ice, and the people skidding in darkness!"

"Ah," said the giant's mother. Nothing more. But she bandaged the whole length of Mandi's golden arm, so that he should not get into trouble with the giant.

Next day, Espereg went out to tend his goats. Before he left, he shut Mandi in the cellar as usual. "No more accidents now, little moppensocks. What a worry you are to your daddy."

Soon as he was gone, Mandi crawled up the cellar steps (the darkness weighed on him like a pile of blankets) and summoning his last scrap of courage, his last dregs of energy, he kicked down the cellar door.

Sun and Moon light tumbled in on him, washing away his disguise, restoring him to the size and shape of a man. Through the fortress he ran, till he found the waterfall. There, planted to right and left, like citrus trees, stood the Sun and the Moon.

Such was the size of that hall in the middle of the fortress that a horse, three yaks and several chickens found ample room to drink at the pool below the waterfall in the centre. With one blazing beacon-basket over each shoulder, Mandi leapt into the horse's saddle.

"Which way now?" he said to himself.

"If you were to ask me," said the horse, "I might recommend trying the third corridor on the left. But before making the attempt, perhaps you might care to put your hand into my left ear and see what you can see."

Mandi reached into the horse's ear and felt the hilt of a sword.

So when, at the castle gate, he met Espereg coming home, he had the means to fight him. "This will be easy," thought Mandi, seeing the giant had no sword.

Not a bit of it.

No sooner had he cut off the giant's head than seven more grew where the old one had been. Ugly, snarling heads they were, the eyes all fixed on the lovely Sun and Moon slung across Mandi's back. With teeth and hands, kicks and shoves, the giant fought for his dearest possessions.

"Mine, poogie-flugle," said one head.

"Give them back, buttonchop," said another.

". . . or I'll bite you to pieces, bulgy bodikin."

". . . stomp you to sausagemeat, moppensocks!"

"Give 'em up or die, toodle-eggy-bumps!"

But the seventh head said nothing, because Mandi had cut it off. And soon, because the horse's sword was magic, five more heads went bouncing away down the mountainside.

"I'm dying, little god Mandi," said Giant Espereg, tumbling like an avalanche down the Hindu Kush.

"For that I am sorry," said Mandi. "You were a good father to me while I was your child. But the world must have warmth and light, must have its Daystar and Nightlight."

"Oh I know! Don't I know!" groaned the dying giant. "How cold I am, and how dark and terrible a place this is to die!" Espereg had fallen to the bottom of a deep gulley, between mountains mildewy and cold. Even before the theft, no light had been able to warm the valley bottom where Espereg now lay shivering.

But Mandi was filled with the magic of the beacons he carried on his back. Restored now to the size and strength of a god, full-grown, he set his shoulder against a mountain and pushed and pummelled and shoved it backwards, so that daylight splashed into the giant's face. "Let the Sun shine on your grave and on your soul, Espereg. Even after you are gone, your golden fortress will prove to the world that here lived a man who understood beauty!"

Espereg sighed. He rolled on to his back, face to the sky, hands tucked up on his chest like a giant sea otter. And with a smile on his last remaining face, he died.

"That was easy," thought Mandi.

Not a bit of it.

Because both Sun and Moon were still across his back, however hard Mandi rode Espereg's horse around the world, half the globe remained steeped in darkness. The half where he rode was dazzled by the brightness, scorched by the heat.

So at last Imra, greatest of all the gods, took from Mandi the beacon-baskets on their iron tripods and flung them out into space. They spun into orbit, spun apart, so that the Sun lit the Day and Moon lit the Night.

No more can men view them up close, those citrus trees of light. Nor can any one god, any one man lay claim to them. They are everyone's to enjoy.

But somewhere within the mossy gorges of the Hindu Kush, there stands a gleaming golden fortress lit by the evening sun. And deep inside it a waterfall still runs, which once watered those citrus trees of light.

The Bridge of Magpies
A Story from China

CHIH NU, daughter of the Sun, worked each night, all night, in the halls of the sky, weaving silk at a loom made of clouds. To and fro, to and fro her shuttle flew, and those who glimpsed it from Earth far below would think they had seen a shooting star. Tapestries of blue silk shot with lilac billowed from her loom — fabric to mend tears in the sky. There were scarlet and orange banners, too, to fly at sunset, and the tissuey shreds of rainbow-coronas which sometimes halo the sun. All these Chih Nu wove, her head down, barely glancing at the universe she helped to deck with her artistry.

"Chih Nu works too hard," said her father, the Sun. "I never hear her laugh, never see her rest. It can't be healthy for a girl of her

47

age to work so hard and relax so little." So he considered how he might cheer his daughter's life. The fiery furnace of his brain soon gave him the answer. Chih Nu should marry!

"Daughter, I have it in mind to find you a husband," said the Sun.

Chih Nu's hands barely faltered over the weft of her weaving. "As my honourable father wishes, so shall it be," she said in a shy whisper. "And if it pleases my honourable father to choose Tung Yung, the cowherd, I should thank him with all my heart."

"*Tung Yung?* My daughter marry a *cowherd*? Oh, surely some princely planet, some collection of stars...!"

But he could see that Chih Nu *had* glanced up from her loom every once in a while, and had seen Tung Yung. Her heart was already set on the handsome drover whose cows graze on the cloudy hillsides at night. "Very well. I give the match my blessing. Marry Tung Yung, my child, and may he teach you that there is more to life than weaving."

Chih Nu thought she would burst with joy. For though only their eyes had ever met, girl and boy had glanced shyly at one another daily for a great many years, and they were deeply in love.

Oh what a wedding that was! Amid a confetti of stardust, the Moon bore in a feast of delicacies all icing-sugar white. The bride wore silk of her own weaving, and the groom a jacket of woven grass reaped from the meadows of midnight. Chih Nu and Tung Yung were so much in love that they barely noticed which guests came, what speeches were made in their honour. They simply gazed into one another's eyes and breathed each other's names, breaths mingling like the haze around twin moons.

As for Chih Nu's loom, it stood abandoned. In the days following the wedding, work never crossed her mind; her thoughts were all of kissing and dancing, listening to Tung Yung and laughing at his jokes. When he went back to tend his cows, she went hand in hand with him and picked flowers for his hair and chased butterflies around hayricks of cloud. The silence of Space was pierced through with Chih Nu's singing, and the Sun began to be anxious all over again.

"When are you going back to your weaving, Daughter?" he asked.

"Oh, later, later!" she would laugh, twirling around, flinging her arms out wide with happiness. "There's more to life than weaving!"

"So that's what your cowherd husband has taught you, is it? A

disregard for duty, a contempt for hard work!"

"No, you—" Chih Nu began to say.

But the Sun was not prepared to listen. There were worn patches and tears in the sky unmended, black holes through which whole clusters of stars kept slipping away. There were no orange gonfalons to deck the Sun's throne, no tissuey silver to braid the Moon's hair.

"That rascal Tung Yung has taught you to be as idle as he is! I knew all along he was the wrong husband for you. Well, it can't go on!"

And he banished Tung Yung to the far side of the Heavenly Silver Stream, a river flowing fast, wide and dangerous through his entire empire of sky. "Back to your loom, child! Back to your cows, Tung Yung! Your marriage is dissolved!"

Marriages can be dissolved. But love? Love can no more be dissolved than a stone in water. Though Chih Nu went back to her loom, she could not count the warps for the trembling of her hands, could not shoot her shuttle or knot her threads for the blinding tears in her eyes. The silk she wove was faulty and snagged, with a puckered selvage and no colour: no colour but the colour of

50

tears. As for Tung Yung, he let his cattle stray among the asteroids and graze on the flowers of the Immortals.

The Sun shook his fiery head. "Ah, daughter, daughter! This cannot be! Listen to the will of your father, and obey it. One day each year, you may cross the Heavenly Silver Stream…"

"Oh!"

"…and spend one day with your husband. But for the rest of the year you must pay attention to your work, for much depends on your weaving – more than I realised before."

"Oh, thank you, Father, thank you! But how? The river is so wide…"

"This is how."

The Emperor Sun whistled softly, and up from the Earth flew every bird ever to put on the black and white livery of a magpie. The magpies flocked towards the Heavenly Silver Stream in such numbers that wings overlapped wings, tails overlapped tails – a million magpies flocking so densely that their bodies formed a solid bridge of speckling black and white, soft under Chih Nu's running feet.

She crossed the Magpie Bridge and flung herself into Tung

Yung's arms, happy for a day, happy all year that this one day of joy awaited her.

But when each year that day approaches, Chih Nu's hands tremble over her loom; her attention is not on her work. If it rains in the Cosmos, the Heavenly Silver Stream will swell and quicken, rise and overspill its banks – a seething torrent of floodwater so violent that the gentle magpies would be swept away in an instant. If the rains begin too early, the magpies do not come. The bridge cannot be formed. And Chih Nu and Tung Yung must wait another whole year to kiss.

Down on Earth, the people of China long since heard tell of the Weaver Maiden and the Cowherd. And every person who ever felt the joy of love, the pain of separation, the sweetness of reunion, watches the sky and prays for fair weather. They lay out fruit and cakes, light perfumed candles, as if for a wedding anniversary, and smile fondly at the thought of Chih Nu leaving her loom, running over the Magpie Bridge, and leaping into her husband's open arms.

Hold your breath: the season of magpies is approaching. Hold out your hand. Was that a drop of rain? It mustn't rain! Not until the magpies have mustered! Not until Chih Nu has crossed over the river…

Orion's Downfall

A Story from Ancient Greece

ORION was a hunter in a time when the world was divided between those who hunted and those who were hunted. Orion, son of the Sea, could shoot an arrow through the curl of a wave, throw a spear from one island kingdom to the next, could bruise the face of the moon with his slingshot and slash the head from monsters. Orion strode the world in league-long, loping strides, his sword-tip dragging a groove in the earth behind him. One blow from his massive warclub could drive a tree into the ground like a tentpeg, shiver a city wall to sand, or knock a boulder into orbit round the sun.

That is why he was the ideal person to rid the Isle of Chios of its wild beast. "I'll do it," said Orion, when King Oenopion asked him, "I'll do it in exchange for the hand of your lovely daughter Merope. Because the love I hold for her in my heart is as great as the strength in my hands."

Oenopion promised his daughter to Orion. He would have promised anything so as to be rid of the gigantic bull terrorising his kingdom. As big as a hill, Taurus shook whole vineyards on the tip of one horn, trampled a grove of lemon trees into a lake of bitter juice, felled stone towers with a single ram of its black brow. Its hooves were blood-stained, and its bellow echoed through the King's nightmares night after night. Desperate for someone to blame, the people of Chios trembled on the brink of rebellion; at any moment they might depose their King for leaving them at the mercy of Taurus the Bull.

Whistling with joy at the thought of his coming marriage, Orion disembarked on the shores of Chios. A second ship moored alongside, carrying his faithful hunting dog Sirius – a hound as fearsome as any wild beast and too big to share a ship with his master. His flapping dewlaps swept the ground, and snuffling Sirius picked up the scent of the bull at once, and started inland. What they had mistaken for thunder was in truth the bellowing of Taurus on the rampage.

When the beast appeared from behind a hill, its horns were snarled with ivy and flags, with shreds of canvas and ships' cables; stone-dust whitened its black hide. Pawing the ground and flaring wet nostrils, it fixed Orion with a beady black eye and lowered its terrible horns.

Orion stood his ground, though even he felt his heart clench like

a fist within him and miss a dozen beats. His grip tightened on his club, and he swiftly glanced to either side of him for somewhere to take cover if he was gored. Not Sirius. Fearlessly, the dog leapt directly at the bull's throat. The great crescents of shining horn sliced the air. The hound's deep-throated bark was cut short, punctured into a howling whine, and the dog hurtled into the air. Up and up flew Sirius, a carcass of reddish fur tossed into the sky.

Enraged, Orion gave a roar louder than any bull's bellow, though it was drowned out by the thunder of galloping hooves as Taurus charged. With a grunt of exertion, Orion swung his club. A tip of horn sharp as a spear sliced through his lion skin and left it hanging by a thread. But the huge club struck the black head below the ear, and though the club shivered to splinters Taurus the Bull was lifted clean off the ground.

Over Orion's head it went, carried by its own momentum over sand dune and treetop, hill and mountain. In a low, somersaulting trajectory, the Great Bull of Chios burst free of Earth's gravity and was impaled against the doors of Heaven by a score of spiky stars.

"The Bull Taurus is dead!" Orion shouted over the iron gates of the King's palace. "And the island is rid of all its wild beasts! Now show me my darling bride, and let's have a wedding here!"

"What bride is that?" came the King's tittering reply. "What wedding? My daughter, you say? There must be some mistake. My daughter Merope is already spoken for. My daughter marry a thuggish giant like you? What can you be thinking of?"

Orion stood in the dying moments of the day, looking up at a new star in the sky brighter than all the rest. He knew its unblinking fire. He knew very well its fierce light. His dog Sirius was looking down at him from Heaven, and there was no brighter gleam in the whole sky than that burning Dog Star. The night howled for Sirius. Orion could only whimper.

Overwhelmed by a crippling sadness, Orion went down to the inn to drink. He drank himself drunk. He drank until he could remember nothing about Merope, nothing about Taurus, nothing about his dead dog. Tomorrow... tomorrow would be soon enough to make Oenopion pay for his broken promise...

Realising his danger, the King seized the opportunity. And while Orion lay in a drunken stupor, powerless to defend himself, Oenopion, pernicious, weaselly Oenopion took a dagger and blinded him.

"O you gods! O you immortal rulers of the world! Help me! Help me! Help me!" Stumbling, hands outstretched, Orion roared his misery at the sky. Without even his dog to guide him, he blundered around Chios, bellowing for either justice or pity. His fumbling fingers traced the open O of cave-mouths in a cliff, and from one of these caves a voice spoke back to him. It was an oracle, a soothsayer, a seer.

"Turn your empty eyes to the rising sun, Orion! Let Helios put his fingers into your eyes, and you shall see again!"

So Orion travelled east, taking his direction from the warmth of the sun on his face or on his back. Wading straits of ocean, clambering over archipelagos, he came at last to the easternmost sea, just before daybreak.

As Helios the sun-god drove his chariot through the Gates of Dawn, he saw the sorry sight of Orion stretched out on the shore, crying in his sleep, but without tears because he had no eyes.

Filled with pity, Helios stretched out his fingers, his sunbeam fingers, and plunged their magic into Orion's empty eyesockets. At once Orion's sight was restored, and he opened his eyes to see the fiery chariot climbing the sky above his head. It seemed to him the most beautiful daybreak in the history of the world.

But that dazzle of sunbeams had kindled a terrible fire in his brain. Orion had been robbed: robbed and tricked and blinded. His dog was dead, his bride denied

him. The fire in his brain smouldered and grew and blazed. He filled up with rage as a tree draws up water from its roots to the very tips of its leaves. By noon Orion was all hatred.

Leaping from island to island, in his haste to reach Chios, he happened to meet Artemis, goddess of the hunt. His words fell sweetly on her ears:

"I'll hunt him! I'll tear him! I'll flay him and flitch him and fillet out his bones!"

"Let me come with you," said Artemis, who loved any kind of hunt. Whatever beast could he be talking about?

"Yes, come! We shall kill him together, you and I! Kill him and his household. Kill him and all his friends!" Hotter and hotter grew Orion's lust for blood, his longing to kill and kill and kill. To be revenged. And Artemis clung tight to his muscular arm, excited, grinning at the prospect of such a hunt.

Panic-stricken, Helios looked on, beckoned the other gods to watch. "Orion is a demi-god, a hero, a miracle of strength! But on the rampage like this he's more dangerous than a dozen giant bulls."

"He must be stopped!"

"Yes, but how?"

With sulphur from the hot springs, with magma from the volcanoes, they fashioned a foe to send against Orion: an insect which wore its skeleton on the outside for armour, a creature the colour of rage and venom. They sent Scorpio. Its front claws were armed with pincers, jagged and vice-like; its crackling tail arched upwards, so that its bulbous black sting overhung its back like a deadly, drooping cusp. Huge as an engine of war, and driven by nothing but blind instinct, Scorpio the Scorpion scuttled across the face of the Earth with a noise like fingernails scrabbling on glass.

It could not feel the heat of the sand as it dug itself a burrow. There it lay, in the path of Orion's rampage, waiting, pincers opening and closing, opening and closing.

At the scent of the giant's skin, its scarlet hinged body arched still farther, and poison oozed from the swollen sting.

"Should we be doing this?" said the gods.

"Must we?"

But Scorpio was already out of its burrow.

Orion felt a jag of pain in his ankle as the pincers closed, another as the sting sank home. He gave a snarl of anger and swung his club, catching Scorpio a blow before it had even recoiled three steps. In the next moment it was lifted into the air with a noise of breaking twigs. Sting parted from tail, claw from leg, abdomen from thorax, and Scorpio hurtled piecemeal into the sky.

Orion reeled. His blood grew hot in his veins, the beats too large for his heart. He felt the strength waste in his muscles, and dropped to his knees, to his hands and knees, on to his side. Overhead, a

vast, exploded scorpion peppered the sky with new stars. Then Orion realised he had been stung and that the venom was in his blood, that his death was already inside him. "Let me not lie under the Scorpion," he said.

Artemis stood over him, shocked, her hands in her hair, screaming and screaming: "*Orion the Hunter is dying!*"

But Orion's story is not over. It is part of another, and that other story is part of his.

The Wonderful Doctor
A Story from Ancient Greece

APOLLO, darling of the Greek gods, was adored by women. He loved a fair few in return, but no one as much as himself. So proud and vain was the golden god that it did not surprise him in the least when women swooned at his feet. What astounded him was the thought that a woman could love anyone *more* than him.

"But I saw them together, I tell you," said Apollo's pet crow one day. "As I flew over. Your lover, Koronis, and a mortal man. Kissing."

"*Kissing!?*"

"Troo-hoo-hoo," whistled the songbird in his sweet, trilling voice, and preened its snow-white feathers.

"My sweetheart? Kissing a mortal?"

"Troo-hoo-hoo," warbled the crow. "Where are you going, master?"

"To kill her!" raged Apollo. And that is what he did.

When, from a terrace of Heaven, he saw in the distance his sweetheart walking alone, her newborn baby in her arms, he laid a golden arrow to his golden bow and let fly.

Even as the arrow left the bow, Apollo had misgivings. "What if that crow of mine lied?"

The arrow whistled through the air, its feather fletches a blur of colour.

"Or made a mistake? What if the man she kissed was a friend – or a relation?"

The arrow hummed on its way like a hornet.

"Dear sweet Koronis! Mother of my child! The child, oh!"

With a thud, the arrow struck home. Koronis reeled and began to fall. Apollo's snowy crow came fluttering from its perch and settled on Apollo's shoulder – "Oh, good shot, master!" – only to be swatted to the ground and stamped on.

"Curse on you, you evil bird! Look what you made me do! I've killed my sweet, innocent Koronis!"

The curse singed his songbird, charred its white feathers and lodged in its throat

like poisonous smoke. From that day on the crow's plumage was inky black, its voice a cracked, hoarse *caawk!* shrieking its innocence.

Apollo meanwhile ran to the side of his falling lover. Dead! And not even the immortal gods of Olympus could fetch a mortal back to life: their magic was too meagre.

But before her baby, falling from her arms, touched the ground, Apollo had caught him.

"Aesculapius, you at least shan't die!" Apollo promised his newborn, mortal son.

He entrusted the baby to Chiron, the good Centaur. Wiser than either mortals or gods, Chiron knew the secrets of Nature and Magic, of Philosophy and Hunting, of a healthy body and a sound mind. Living in a hillside cave, he knew the use of every herb growing there, every magic spring. All this he taught to the little boy Aesculapius, and the boy proved a good student.

Nothing he was taught did he forget. Nothing he learned but he found out more for himself, experimenting, exploring, asking questions. By the time he was grown, Aesculapius knew more than Chiron about curing illness, healing injuries, caring for the sick.

"He is a born doctor," the Centaur told Apollo. "See the traffic moving along the roads? See the crowds outside my cave? People are coming from miles around to ask his help. And see their faces when they come out again – cured, happy!"

Not just people visited Aesculapius, either. Animals wounded by hunters, birds mauled by cats, flowers with curling, mildewed leaves, fig trees empty of fruit all came to him for help.

Even the gods.

"Aesculapius, come quickly! Please! At once!"

It was Artemis, Apollo's sister, goddess of hunting. "Oh please, nephew! A young man – such a marvellous, handsome boy – over there! There has been a terrible accident!"

So Aesculapius snatched up his wallet of herbs and tinctures, his cotton bandages, his ointments and balms, his splints and compresses. He washed his magically skilful hands, picked up his magic wand, the one coiled with a double helix of stingless snakes.

At the foot of a cliff lay a giant of a man: Orion the Hunter, dead from the bite of a scorpion. The sea's foam lifted and turned his head, each wave giving the impression he was stirring. But Orion was dead. Orion lay dead because the gods had been afraid of his temper, too afraid to let him live.

But Artemis tore at her hair, struck her open hand against the cliff, crying open-mouthed and silently. The sky itself quaked with horror, with the groans and sighs of the immortal gods, all wishing the thing undone. Artemis piled her long hair in the young doctor's lap and clung to his sleeve. "Orion was the marvel of the world. Orion could shoot an arrow through the curl of a wave, throw a spear from island to island, bruise the moon with his slingshot. Fetch him back to life, nephew! Do it! I'll give you any fee you ask!"

It was not the offer of a reward. Aesculapius felt the genius shout in his blood, the magic of wisdom, the power of perfect knowledge. Unpacking his wallet, he laid out on the ground a garden of herbs, a mosaic of petals and leaves, berries and sepals. He unpacked phials of aquamarine, opalescent, glittering suspensions; gnarled roots and staining pollens; golden liquor from the honey bee, the magic wand coiled with a double helix of stingless snakes.

With these he anointed the dead Orion, bathed his eyes, massaged his limbs. Then, breathing three times into his mouth, and beating three times on the silent heart, he coaxed and cajoled, teased and bullied the spirit of Life back into the cold, limp body.

Orion stirred. Orion groaned. Orion drew breath. And high upon the purple peak of Mount Olympus, the King of the gods, Almighty Zeus, watched as the world's first doctor brought a dead man back to life.

"This cannot be," he said under his breath. "Death must be the end. There can be no coming back.

"This cannot be," said Zeus aloud. "See how the spirits in the Underworld pass the news along; see them jostle for a place near the banks of the Lethe, wanting to come back, wanting to live again.

"This cannot be," said Zeus, raising his voice so that all the gods of Heaven heard him. "The world will soon teem with people, climbing over one another like ants in the nest; not enough food, not enough room …

"THIS CANNOT BE!" said Zeus, so loud that the whole world heard him. "HE HAS MORE MAGIC THAN

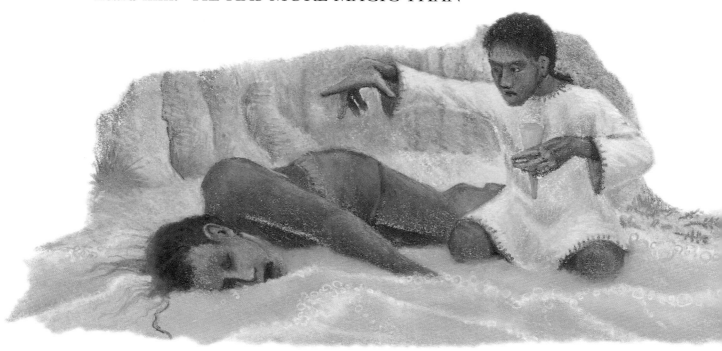

THE GODS! AESCULAPIUS MUST DIE!" And clawing a thunderbolt out of the clouds, he hurled it at the good doctor, sprawled him cold and lifeless among his life-giving medicines.

For a second time, Apollo stood over a dead mortal and wept. He seethed with anger against murdering Zeus. He picked up his son's magic wand and hurled it, meaning to knock from his mountain pinnacle the King of the gods, for killing his brilliant son.

The wand missed, of course, and its momentum carried it on outwards through clouds and stratosphere, into the dark void of space – a rod entwined with a double helix of snakes.

There it hangs in the night sky, healing the ills of those starry constellatory heroes who hang for ever in the soft black, picked out in stars. And from the starry wand, the powdery dust of genius trickles, on to the Earth beneath, on to the eyes of men and women, on to their hands, their open books, the herbs growing at their feet. It must be so. Or where would all the doctors and nurses and healers have come from who now ply the trade of Aesculapius among the sick and the suffering?

Orion, meanwhile, stirred amid the sea's foam. He sat up, confused, slow-witted. The gods held their breath.

What when he remembered the wrong King Oenopion had done him? What when he found out who had sent the scorpion to sting

him? What when he recalled Merope and his dead dog Sirius?
What when he learned of the fate of the doctor who had brought
him back to life? Orion, in his rage, would hunt down every man
and beast in Creation, put an end to the world.

So Zeus dissolved the mortal part of Orion into his father's sea
foam, and pinned his immortal part, with stars, to the heavens.

Now it looks as if Scorpio the Scorpion is for ever scuttling up
towards the giant to deliver its lethal sting. But Scorpio – and
Taurus beyond him – are only exploded voids, whereas Orion lives
on. Hung around his waist by the gods is a belt, a golden trophy
denoting the greatest hunter who ever lived. And panting at his
heels is Sirius, his eager eye the brightest star in all the heavens.

The Giant Under the House
A Story from Guatemala

The world was passing from the time of Giants to the time of the Inca. Only two giants remained – brothers called Mountain-Maker and Earth-Quaker. The brothers had emerald teeth, coarse manners and appetites as huge as their gigantic bodies. And that made them a nuisance.

You know how it is: you are just building a house, a town, a civilisation and along comes a giant. He picks off a roof to wear as a hat, grabs up a handful of cows for his lunch, drinks your river dry. Besides, Mountain-Maker and Earth-Quaker moved the countryside about such a lot. One morning you looked out of your

72

door at a view of quiet fields and gentle hills, the next some towering craggy mountain peak was blocking out the sun and the ground was shaking itself like a blanket, with houses flying hither and thither.

Hero Xbalanque undertook to rid the Earth of these giants. He poisoned Mountain-Maker with roast bird cooked in toxic mud. That only left Earth-Quaker.

"Here's the plan," said Xbalanque to the young men of his village. "I want you to dig a pit – a mighty pit. Then fell some trees – acres of them, I tell you – enough for a house with a hundred rooms and thirty storeys tall. Stack the logs on the edge of the hole, and then cut more, the same number again."

While the young men did this, Xbalanque went looking for the tallest tree in the forest and cut it down. It fell from morning till evening, so far had it to fall.

When he heard Earth-Quaker coming, Xbalanque took hold of a single branch and pulled on it. *Heave!*

"What you doing, personlet?" asked the giant. "And why such a great tree for such a small man?"

"It's the centrepost to hold up the roof of our new meeting house," said Xbalanque, still hauling on the branch. "Any chance you might help me carry it?"

"Well certainly, manling," said Earth-Quaker. "My pleasure." Up went the tree over his shoulder, as easy as a rower carrying his oar. Xbalanque led the way to the village clearing and Earth-Quaker followed behind him, bringing along the tree. "Ooh! What's the big hole for, human-kinder?" asked the giant, seeing the deep-dug pit.

"Foundations, of course, for the house," said Xbalanque. "If we can just set the centrepost deep enough in the ground, and hold it upright with rocks, in no time we shall have a house higher than any house before it. See all the logs we've cut to make the walls? When it's finished, this building will house a hundred men."

"Too poky for me," said the giant. "But it's a good idea. Foundations, eh? Novel."

It was not hard to persuade Earth-Quaker to go down into the hole and to set the centrepost of the house upright. His great hands all but circled the huge trunk, and his two feet held it firm. "Is this how you mean?" asked the obliging giant.

"*NOW!*" cried hero Xbalanque with a yelp of triumph, the excitement hot in his belly.

A hundred young men ran to the pile of logs, the huge timber stack, and knocked away the chocks at the base. The logs began to roll – to roll and slip and spill into the pit. A cataract of hardwood, an avalanche of timber tumbled with a cacophony of banging, end-on, side-on, end-over-end, in on top of Earth-Quaker.

When the noise stopped – silence. No groaning, no roaring, no groping hand reaching through the woodpile to claw at the ambushers. Just a pit filled to the brim with timber – and somewhere beneath them, a dead giant. A hundred young men danced victorious around the pit, whooped and hugged and cheered Xbalanque, their hero.

Then they ran to a second woodpile, as big as the first, and began to build. They built a house with a hundred rooms, and thirty storeys high. And when it was done, there was no house to match it from the western seaboard to the eastern coast. How they sang, those hundred dancing fellows:

"We snared us a giant
Who shook down mountains,
Who juggled hills
And drank down fountains
His name was Earth-Quaker,
Earth-Shaker,
Earth-Breaker.
We tricked him and licked him,
We trapped him and snapped him
Like a rotten piece of wood.
Are we not brave and good?"

Down in the pit, Earth-Quaker heard them singing. Above his head his great hands still gripped the centrepost. As the timber rained down on him, he had jammed the huge trunk across the hole from edge to edge, and sheltered beneath its broad trunk. Crouched now in this sealed cavity at the bottom of the pit, his huge bulk curled into a ball, Earth-Quaker felt the blood drip from his battered fingers. Drink spilled by the partying youths trickled down and dripped on his head. And he had to listen to them singing:

"We crushed him!
We bust him!
We tipped a forest on his head!
And now the evil giant is dead!
That trouble maker,
That Earth-Quaker!"

All day Earth-Quaker
listened, until at last the song
fell silent. He could smell the
remnants of their feast. He knew
that it was dark now in the house overhead –
almost as dark as down here, in his man-made grave.

Curling back his lips, Earth-Quaker bared his
emerald teeth and bit – crunch, spit, snap, spit, crack
– through the wedged centrepost. Then, gathering all
his strength, bracing the aching muscles of his bent
back, Earth-Quaker…STOOD UP.

A million straws of thatch were tossed into outer orbit, making a yellow haze around the Moon. A thousand logs of timber were flung up like husks from a winnowing floor, up into the forests of space.

And, of course, the hundred young men were hurled, like seeds from a poppyhead, looping and somersaulting into thirty storeys of Night. Each woke from a heavy sleep to find himself hurtling upwards, the world a diminishing disc below: small as a pond, small as a pan, small as a pea. But by the time they stopped hurtling upwards, they were so high that they clutched desperately at Nothingness to keep from falling back down, down, down.

And there they crouch to this day, huddled together on the shelves of Night, waiting for the chance to get down, climb down, for someone to carry them down.

Xbalanque is not among them. If he had been, there might still be giants on the Earth today. Earth-Quaker might still lumber through the forests of Guatemala like a man through tall grass, might still smile his emerald smile and wave a genial smile at the people far below. But Xbalanque was not in the house that night.

He has yet to work out how to fetch down the hundred young men whose eyes glitter reproachfully at him out of the night sky. Still, he has had his successes. See the emerald necklace round his throat. Now where do you suppose he got that?

The Heat of the Moment

A Story from the Cook Islands

ONCE, when brothers and sisters never quarrelled, there were twins who loved each other more than most. Some days it seemed to their mother that Tiri and Piri needed no one but each other. For all she loved them, that gave her a strange, shut-out feeling, a feeling she did not like.

One evening their mother took a torch and went gathering shellfish in the rockpools along the seashore. Hour after backbreaking hour she paddled and dabbled and scrabbled for limpets and mussels to feed the family. By the time she had enough for a meal, it was the middle of the night.

Now shellfish taste best fresh for the sea. So she set to work to cook them at once, even though her husband and children had long since gone to sleep. And so vexing was it to her, hearing their steady peaceful breathing as she worked, that she worked herself into more and more of a rage.

"Why do I take all this trouble? Fishing for them. Cooking for them. What thanks do I get? What appreciation? None! When do I get to sleep? When does anyone give me a helping hand? Not Tiri, he's too wrapped up in Piri. Not Piri, she's too busy playing with Tiri. They take me for granted, the whole pack of them! An unpaid cook, that's me!"

By the time the shellfish were simmering in the pan, she was fairly dancing with rage. "Get up, you idle so-and-so!" she told her husband, giving him a kick. "Get up and eat your supper!"

"Huh? Uh? Oh, right. I'll wake the children," he said blearily.

"Let 'em sleep. Let 'em starve for all I care!" said the mother, in the heat of the moment.

But her angry voice had already woken little Piri. She woke to the sound of her mother saying "Let 'em starve!"

"You don't mean that," said the children's father soothingly.

"Don't I? They bring me nothing but work and grief, that pair." (Mothers often say terrible things in the heat of the moment.)

"Wake up, brother!" Piri whispered to her brother. "We have to run away. Hear how Mother hates us! Says she wishes we were dead. We can't stay here!"

Tiri was afraid. But so long as he had Piri by his side, he dared anything. "I'll take care of you in the great wide world!" he declared bravely.

"And I'll take care of you," she replied, taking his hand.

Out they crept, towards the beach, towards the bright light which signified the sea. But the waves hissed at them, unfriendly and fearsome in the dark. Along the beach they walked, but the crabs rattled at them and seaweed crackled under their feet. They wandered to the very end of the beach, and as they walked it dawned on them how foolish they had been.

Their home was an island, hemmed in by sea. Where could they possibly go?

"It's hopeless," said Tiri as they sat on the rocks at the end of the beach. "We have to go back home."

"And be beaten for running away? Or starve, because our mother doesn't want us? Never! We have to go on!" said Piri.

Tears ran down their faces and dropped on to the hard, unforgiving rocks.

"But there *is* nowhere to run," said Tiri.

"Oh yes there is – if we dare!" said Piri.

The night sky hung down like a swag of black canvas, an awning of dark so close they could almost reach up and touch it.

"I dare if you dare," said Piri.

"I dare if you dare," said Tiri.

So Piri stood up and leapt. Behind her jumped Tiri, her brother. Leaping into the night sky, snatching hold, scrambling and scrabbling up the steep chute of black, they climbed past moon and planets.

★

An hour later, and the sky began to pale as the sun stirred below the horizon.

"Get up, husband! The children are gone!" cried a woman's voice in a house near the sea.

Father and mother stumbled into the garden, calling, searching, "Tiri! Piri?" They looked among the palm trees and inland among the dark undergrowth. They called out to sea and up into the treetops. But Tiri and Piri had disappeared.

Their parents ran along the tide-washed sand, as far as the rocks at the end of the beach, and found the boulders puddled with saltwater – not brine but tears. Aghast, they looked out at the rolling waves.

"Come back! I didn't meant it!" called their mother, weeping still more tears.

"Come back! We love you dearly!" called their father, but even his big voice did not carry over the hiss of the surf.

"Drowned?" sobbed their mother, beating her head on the rocks.

"No! " exclaimed their father, pointing upwards. "*Flying!* See?"

There hung two new stars in the sky, so pale in the glowing, growing dawn that they were barely visible. But the parents did not hesitate one moment. They leapt, one after the other, as high as hope would lift them – and ran after their children across

the rag-end of night.

Each time Tiri and Piri look back, they see that they are being chased. But thinking it is anger which brings their mother running after them, they run on, hand in hand, as fast as they can run. So, day in, night out, their parents run after them, never closing the gap, but never giving up their chase. Because they must explain, they have to explain…

"We didn't meant it! We love you!"

And just as a mother's and father's love for their children never ends, neither will the chase of those desolate parents hurrying after the Inseparable Twins, calling, calling.

The Many-Coloured Llama
A Story from Peru

PACHA was a good man, though he did not have much to
show for it – hardly more than his llama. Oh, he had a wife
and children, too, but he hardly ever saw them, for he was always
walking – up mountain, down mountain – at the side of his llama,
steadying her heavy load. Together they fetched goods, carried
goods, delivered goods from village to town, mountaintop to
valley bottom. And wherever they went they saw crime and
wickedness, cruelty and greed, ugliness and sin. Mouths spat at
them, sneered at them, cursed and shrieked at them: never smiled
or called a blessing. Pacha had to wait until he got home to see a
smile on the face of his children, to hear sweet words from the lips

of his wife. He tended not to look at mouths any more.

So he was startled one day when, as he walked – up mountain, down mountain – he heard someone say, "Beware, Pacha!"

Pacha looked around. There was nothing to see but the flower-strewn slopes of a Peruvian mountainside. He shrugged and gave a tug on the llama's halter. "Let's go home, Vacana. Trot on."

"There's a flood coming, Pacha," said the voice again.

Pacha looked around. Who could have spoken? Unless…

"Build a boat, Pacha," said Vacana, nodding her silken head, forming the words with her soft, puckered lips. "The world has grown wicked. The great god Ilyap'a is sending a flood to wipe out Mankind. You alone are a good man. We llamas can judge such things. So build a boat – and do it quickly. There's not much time left."

So, no sooner did Pacha reach home than he began to build a boat – even though he lived hundreds of metres high on a Peruvian mountainside. He worked while the sun shone, while the clouds gathered. Crowds gathered, too, of miscellaneous animals, birds and insects. They stood about him, patient, waiting, summoned by instinct to their saviour: Pacha the llama man. Pacha hammered on as the first drizzle fell. Even so, his boat was barely finished before rain fell from the springs of the sky in cataracts, as if emptied from a bucket over Peru's head.

And though the mountains of Peru bang their heads against the sky, such a flood arose that the water swallowed everything, submerged everything, washed away everything. Orchards, farmland, markets, graves disappeared under boiling torrents of muddy water, setting Pacha's boat afloat, lifting it lurchingly over

the treetops of inundated forests. What a strange menagerie there was aboard that little ark! Pacha, his wife, his children, and all those birds and beasts, with nothing to do but ride – up wave, down wave – over the interminable flood, nothing to look at but the sun by day and the stars by night.

At last the flood subsided, uncovering a sodden, strangely empty Earth. It was time to disembark, to scatter, to explore the new world – up mountain, down mountain – choosing places to build anew nests and dens and homes.

Only once more did Vacana speak to Pacha (though he spoke to her and stroked her every single day). Pacha was busy prising apart the planks of the ark, to build a fire to cook supper on, and to fend off the fearful weight of starry darkness. Vacana paused for a moment, in chewing the cud, to say, "Look up, Pacha! Ilyap'a has set his llama loose to graze. Look up, Pacha, and see the beautiful Orqo-Cilay!"

Pacha looked up. There among the menagerie of starry constellations, a handful of stars – some glimmering redly, some a little blue – pricked out the shape of a giant llama grazing on the thistly stars. He breathed in a breath of wonder, and his hands slipped the halter from Vacana's head, turning her loose for ever.

Each night, Ilyap'a sets Orqo-Cilay loose to graze, and each night the many-coloured, silken-haired llama trots – up black mountain, down dark dale – across the sky and mysteriously out of sight. She has gone to drink at the Catachillay spring, watersource of Heaven. So long as she drinks, the night can never overbrim and flood the world below. Small wonder that the descendants of Pacha watch out for the many-coloured llama, and smile with relief to see it there, nibbling on the tussocks of night sky.

The Cockatoo and the White Gum Tree
An Aboriginal Story from Australia

THE yellow-crested cockatoo, in the morning of the world, sat in the white gum tree with her tailplumes unfurled. Under the branch where she perched, First Man sat resting, weary from walking.

The yellow-crested cockatoo gave a shrill, scornful laugh. "Look at you! You limp and crawl and trudge about the Earth, while I? I fly! There you sit, on the sun-crazed, thorny desert, with no one but the ants for company and nothing to eat but cactus meat, while I? I sing in this white gum tree."

Woolly-headed First Man shielded his eyes against the sun and looked up into the tree. "We live where the Creator put us," he replied quite simply. "Cactus meat is sweet, and so is life, for all he gave *you* the white gum tree to sit in."

Now, a little higher up, in the sky above the white gum tree, sat the Creator, planning and making and musing about what else needed to be made. He had already invented Death, and held it in the palm of his left hand, though he had not, as yet, told First Man or First Woman of his invention. It was time he did.

So as soon as the yellow-crested cockatoo flew off to a waterhole to drink, Creator said to First Man, "I never meant this life of yours to go on for ever. See here – in my left hand – I have a present for you. Take it. It was always meant for you."

The yellow-crested cockatoo stayed drinking and preening herself by the waterhole until the heat went out of the day. As the sky was turning to ink, she flew back to roost in the white gum tree.

At least she flew to where the white gum tree had stood that morning. But on the spot where her tree had been, she found no spreading branches, no First Man, nothing and no one in fact,

though she could hear, through the darkness, First Woman and First Children crying, lamenting, mourning. Up and down she flew, up and down, searching for her beautiful white gum tree; but it was nowhere to be found. Soon the yellow-crested cockatoo was forced to land on the ground and drag her tailplumes through the red desert dust.

Then, looking up, she saw what Creator had done. There in the dark sky hung one more silver constellation than the night before: her beautiful white gum tree. Its leaves were stars, its roots still clogged with soft, black soil. And there, among the branches, sat First Dead Man, curled up and contentedly watching; watching the isles, the icecaps, the restless oceans, the shifting desert dunes of the world from his starry look-out.

With a shriek of jealous rage, the yellow-crested cockatoo flapped into the air, beat with her wings to gain height, stretched out her neck and yearned towards the white gum tree. Higher and higher she flew, meaning to topple her rival from his delectable perch. But though she flew and she flew, though she is flying still – though she herself climbed so high that her feathers became stars and her body a constellation – she has never reached her goal. And now, when she peers ahead of her at her sweet white gum tree, she can see that its boughs are crowded with ghosts, with happy, smiling, woolly-haired ghosts – our ancestors – chattering and laughing and watching over the children they left behind among the fruiting cactus plants.

95

Great Bear, Little Bear
A Story from Ancient Rome

THOUGH many stories begin with Love, this one is born out of Hate – the hatred that Diana felt for men.

Diana was a goddess. Diana was a huntress. But unlike the other gods on Olympus, unlike the other, mortal hunters in the forest, Diana never hunted a mate. All men, she said, were fools and weaklings.

She surrounded herself instead with maids-in-waiting, unmarried wood nymphs and water sprites who swore never to marry, never to waste a glance or a kiss on any worthless male. For Diana despised men. Perhaps because she could run faster, shoot straighter, think with more cunning, she could not see what in the world men and boys were good for.

Callisto was her favourite little handmaid –
so pretty, so sweet-natured, such a useful,
helpful girl. So the day that Callisto betrayed
her, there was no end to Diana's fury.

"You have grown fat, Callisto," said Diana.
"How have you grown so fat?"

"Eating oranges, mistress," Callisto lied.

"Your cheeks are red, Callisto," said
Diana. "Why are you blushing?"

"I, I –" Callisto was not practised in
lying, and she could find no place on
her big, blossoming body to hide this
particular lie one day longer. "I am
expecting a baby, mistress – the child of
Jupiter, King of the gods. I tried to say no
to his offer of love – truly I did! – but how
can a humble nymph like me say no to the
King of the gods?"

Just then the baby in Callisto's womb
kicked and struggled to be free. Diana, her
face as white and frosty and
bleak as snow, watched as her
handmaid gave birth to a son.
Then she held out the palm of
one hand, as if to blot out the
sight, and said, "Callisto, you
are a traitor to the sisterhood of

Diana. You have given your love to a wretched man when you promised it always and only to me. Be gone from my company of women. But don't think that any paltry man will have you instead of me. Those cowards will run away from the very sight of you – or hunt you down and shoot you. Now run, or I shall shoot you myself!"

Callisto ran. She clutched up her newborn son and she ran. But she found she could not run on two legs, only on four, the knuckles of one hand to the ground while the other cradled her son, a loping stride and her breath coming in great gruff sobs. Around her shoulders swung a shawl of thick fur, along her arms a silky pelt; she gouged the earth with long, slashing claws. Diana had turned her into a bear!

For days Callisto cowered in a cave, her little boy cradled in the long soft fur of her lap. And while she hid, she considered her plight. What kind of life could she, a she-bear give to a human baby? What kind of home or care or joy?

"I give you the name of Artus, little one," she said, her voice a low growl of misery. "But what else can I give you? I will entrust you to the care of your father, Jupiter the Almighty. May you live long, find fame and think well of the mother you never knew. It breaks my heart to part from you, but I must roam where the bears roam, and you must grow up among men and women."

What did Jupiter do? He did not countermand the magic of Diana, though he had enough magic in any one of his fingers. He did not tell the boy Artus, as he grew, the sad story of his mother, did not confess to being Artus' father. But he did see to it that the boy never went hungry, never wanted for a place to live or a good

reputation. In fact he made him King of Arcadia. And watching him from the slopes of Heaven, he grew rather fond of the boy.

Like every other girl in the sisterhood of Diana, Callisto had been a huntress, and Artus inherited her skill. He could shoot an arrow into the heart of a deer at a thousand paces, could stalk a rabbit through snow without leaving a footprint, track a boar through water. And he would kill bears, too.

One day, when he was about sixteen, Artus was out hunting in the Forest of Arcadia. As he chased a stag on foot, the creature leapt into a clearing and immediately sheared away into thick woodland.

For there, devouring a honeycomb, sat a huge old long-tailed bear. Artus was running too fast to stop. He skidded into the clearing and came face to face with the bear.

Callisto looked up and snarled, thinking to protect her honey. Her claws slid from their furred sheaths. But one look at Artus and she withdrew her claws, bit back her growl. There was no mistaking him. He had her eyes, her one-time texture of hair, the family nose, her frame, her face.

Artus summed up the gnarled old bear. A female. They are the most dangerous. He tried to judge her mood. Had she eaten her fill? Could he step back among the trees without her coming after him? He saw the lower jaw sag open, saw the bear rise to her hind feet. Artus cursed his luck. She was about to charge!

Callisto stood up on her hind legs and spread wide her arms. Surely her son would realise – must realise – who she was and how overjoyed she was to see him! To hold him in her arms again! Oh, to clasp him to her chest!

Artus had seen men killed by bears, gripped in the monstrous grasp and hugged to death against a furry chest. Carefully, without letting his arms move, he drew an arrow from his quiver with only the fingers of one hand. Once it was in his grip, he could lay it to his bow or plunge it into the bear's belly as she pounced…

"Oh, Artus! Artus, my beloved son! At last you have found me!" cried Callisto (though the words came out as a deafening growl).

On top of Mount Olympus, Jupiter watched with horrid fascination the meeting of mother and son. He saw what was about to happen, knew that either son would kill mother or mother son. He pictured Callisto's grief, her wet black nose sniffing at the corpse

she had inadvertently crushed in her arms, her giant paw turning him over and over...

"No!"

Jupiter took one step. He took two more. Between the moment when Callisto lurched towards her son and Artus' fist closed round his arrow, Jupiter strode down from Mount Olympus and caught hold of Callisto's tail. He swung her once, twice, three times around his head, then hurled her into the sky.

Artus stared, mouth open, arrow dropping from his grasp.

"She was your mother!" panted Jupiter, resting his hands on his knees after the exertion of such a throw. "The mother who bore you and the mother who would have hugged you to death in a passion of tenderness!"

Looking up, Artus saw it was true. For a bear, its pelt aglitter with stars, was even now climbing up the darkening sky with a terribly, solitary prowl, starry eyes fastened on the Earth.

"Let me go with her!" said Artus impulsively. "One moment I find my mother, the next I've lost her again. Let me go with her! Please!"

Jupiter thought for only a moment before nodding. He snatched hold of Artus' long-tailed jacket, whirled him round and let go, just as a stevedore heaves a sack on board a ship.

A moment later, not one but two bears – a large female and one hardly more than a cub – were cantering nimbly up the sky.

"Wait for me, Mother! Wait for me!"

Each time she saw those two bears, Diana would try to laugh her most spiteful laugh, try to revel in the punishment she had inflicted on her treacherous handmaid. But the companionable closeness of those two wandering bears, loping in a circle around the North Star, planted a pain somewhere in her childless heart and filled her with longing for something she had never had.

Even now, when no shrines still stand to the goddess Diana, people the world over point to the constellations of Ursa Major and Ursa Minor and say, "Look, the Great Bear! And there beside it – the Little Bear! Always together in the sky."

The Watched Pot

A Basque Story from Spain

MORE like a saucepan than a bear, say the Spanish Basques, as the light fails and the seven stars of Ursa Major begin to glow and throb. More like a saucepan catching the reflections of sunset's fire, steadied by an invisible hand.

Old Man Alcor set it over the fire on the first day of Time. Pausing to rest on his walk to Infinity, he set his saucepan to heat. The planets gathered round his head like blowflies, but he did not stir to swat them away. The firefly stars glimmered, but he did not notice them. His eyes were fixed on the pan and on its contents.

Hunkered down, his head between his knees, balancing on the balls of his feet, Alcor continues to sit, muttering softly to himself or humming between lips puckered with age. Celestial

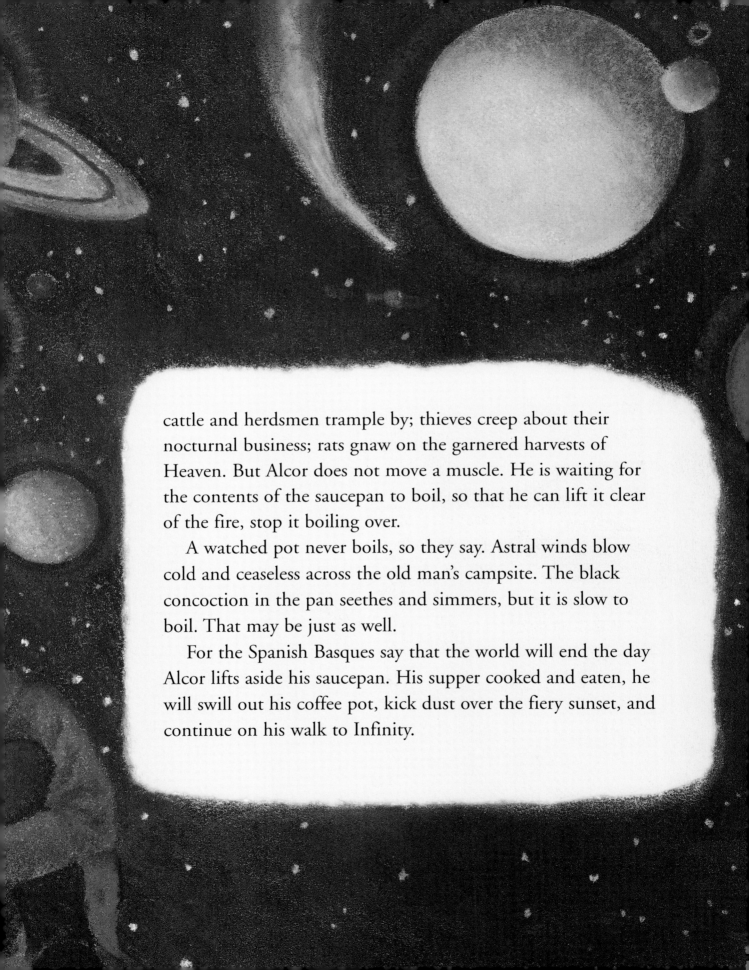

cattle and herdsmen trample by; thieves creep about their nocturnal business; rats gnaw on the garnered harvests of Heaven. But Alcor does not move a muscle. He is waiting for the contents of the saucepan to boil, so that he can lift it clear of the fire, stop it boiling over.

A watched pot never boils, so they say. Astral winds blow cold and ceaseless across the old man's campsite. The black concoction in the pan seethes and simmers, but it is slow to boil. That may be just as well.

For the Spanish Basques say that the world will end the day Alcor lifts aside his saucepan. His supper cooked and eaten, he will swill out his coffee pot, kick dust over the fiery sunset, and continue on his walk to Infinity.

About the Stories

Starbright, Starspite

To the Pawnee tribes of Nebraska, North America, Tirawa is an unpredictable Creator, prone to fits of rage. But in this story, which explains how Death was set loose on Earth, the stars and not Tirawa are to blame for the disaster.

The Bat and the Basket

African myths almost invariably make use of animals and birds. This one, from Sierra Leone, is told by the Kono people, both to explain why the moon is less bright than the sun, and why, at dusk, the sky is filled by teeming millions of bats.

Shooting Stars

Nowadays, we look on a shooting star as a chance to make a wish (although we know it is just a meteorite burning up in Earth's atmosphere). It was not always an omen of good luck. Once it foretold the death of a friend, or famous person. In this Arabian story the stars are the spears of the angels – angels of Allah, the One True God of the Moslem religion.

Divorce

It is, of course, far too simple to say that the moon shines at night, the sun in the daytime. Quite often, a ghostly white moon can be seen high in a blue, sunlit sky. This myth from Togo, West Africa, tackles the reason why, and, in doing so, accounts for the glorious phenomenon of rainbows.

The Devil's Worst Invention

This story is a French folktale. The mundane scientific reason, of course, why we see lightning before we hear thunder is that light travels faster than sound.

The Giant Who Stole the Sun

To the Prasun Kafir people of the Hindu Kush mountains, Afghanistan, Mandi is a lesser god than Imra the supreme deity, but more of a hero-warrior. According to them, Mandi disposed of the troublesome giants who inhabited the world before us, in time for his fellow gods to create people, animals, tools, weapons and agriculture.

The Bridge of Magpies

Star worship is still very much practised in China, where Taoists believe the stars control love, health, wealth and the weather. Stars, they believe, give rise to war or peace, command the angels and demons, and decide the fates of men and women. Chih Nu is the star we call Vega; Tung Yung we know as the constellation of Aquila the Eagle.

Orion's Downfall

Orion, as old as the most ancient of Greek myths, has always been associated with storms; as his starry head rises into the northern hemisphere, winter weather begins. At his feet sits Sirius, the Dog Star. As the constellation of the Scorpion rises in spring, Orion fades, as if dying. He sinks into the Underworld with his dog until autumn restores him to life. In Ancient Babylon, the same glittering star-giant was worshipped as the god of precious gems.

The Wonderful Doctor

Aesculapius is kept company in the night sky by his centaur guardian Chiron – the zodiacal sign Sagittarius. Long after his Greek cult became established, the Romans introduced the worship of Aesculapius, and his 'priests' passed on their healing skills to their sons as sacred secrets. Most Roman doctors were, in fact Greeks.

The Giant Under the House

So many stories are told about the Pleiades that it is hard to choose one. This Guatemalan myth sees the star cluster as a group of house builders blasted into the sky. Elsewhere it is a group of sisters chased there by Orion the hunter, or seven greedy sons who turned into stars because their mother would not feed them enough. In the tropics, their rising is associated with the coming of the rainy season.

The Heat of the Moment

The brother and sister in this story are known to the Cook Islanders as the Inseparables. In Western astrology, they are Castor and Pollux or Gemini the Twins, devoted brothers who refused to be separated by death. Their pairing in the sky has given rise to 'twin' myths in Asia, Australia, Europe and Polynesia.

The Many-Coloured Llama

Orqo-Cilay means 'constellation of the many-coloured llama'. The stars we call Alpha and Beta Centauri are, to the Techwas Indians of Peru, 'the eyes of the llama'. The Catachillay Spring where Orqo-Cilay drinks are the Pleiades.

The Cockatoo and the White Gum Tree

A constellation of the southern hemisphere, the White Gum Tree is seen
by Australian aboriginal people as the roosting place of the spirits of their dead
ancestors. To these people, so in tune with their environment, the night sky is simply
an extension of the Australian Bush. The Southern Cross, most distinctive
of the southern constellations, is known to the aborigines as the Eagle's Nest.

Great Bear, Little Bear

Some versions of this Roman myth, concerning the star groups Ursa Major and Ursa
Minor, picture not mother bear and cub, but Bootes the Bear-keeper, eternally
driving the bear Callisto round the Pole Star with a whip.
To the Egyptians, the constellation of Ursa Major was the likeness of Osiris, the
bright star Cirrus representing his wife Isis. (See also "The Watched Pot" below).

The Watched Pot

Alcor shines at the end of the handle of the Plough, or Big Dipper, or Casserole,
or halfway down the tail of the Great Bear – depending on what you term this most
distinctive group of stars. The Spanish Basques, in common with the French,
view it as a saucepan, in a myth which, oddly, entrusts to a pale and minor star
the fate of the entire world.

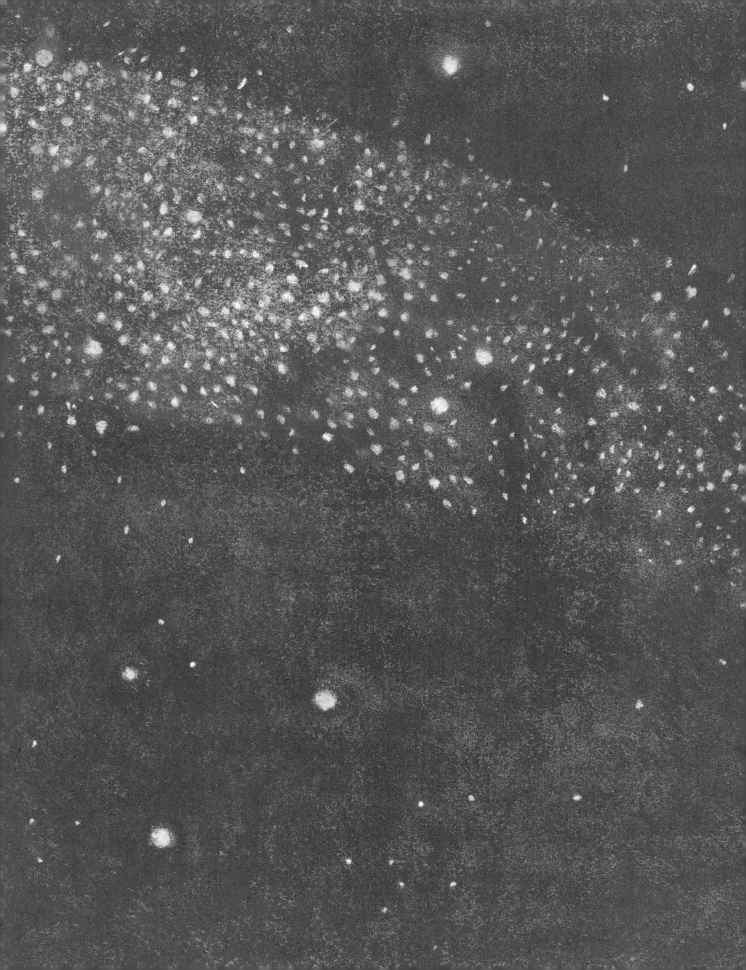